Journeys Near and Far

A Collection of
Memoirs, Poetry and Intrigue

by the
Essex County
Consortium Students

Congratulations, a
fire story—
4x

[signature]

Journeys Near and Far -A Collection of Memoirs, Poetry and Intrigue

By the Essex County Consortium Students,

Copyright © 2017 By Essex County Consortium.

Edited by Judith Celestin, Ellen Ray and Rebecca Feit-Klein.

Produced by Hard Ball Press for the Essex County Consortium.

Information available at: www.hardballpress.com

ISBN: 978-0-9979797-7-0

Cover art by Davidson Beneche (Essex County College student from the Adult Learning Center)

Exterior and interior book design by D. Bass

Dedication

To all the nontraditional students who are enrolled in adult education programs, to those who have difficulty writing, to those who may love to write, and to our teachers and funder (New Jersey Department of Labor & Workforce Development), we dedicate these stories

Journeys Near and Far

A Collection of
Memoirs, Poetry and Intrigue

by the
Essex County
Consortium Students

Edited by Judith Celestin and Ellen Ray

Contents

Introduction

The students who contributed their poems and stories to this book dared to share their hopes and dreams. Once they accepted the challenge to write, they put pen to paper, reaching into their history and experience with a desire to "know what will come out at the end of the story."

At times, our students say that they do not know what or how to write. Writing does not come as easily as they would like. However, I know that each of them has a story to tell and has had various experiences that have made them the resilient people they are today.

As Director of the Adult Learning Center, I am always looking to assist our students in improving or developing their writing skills in fun and creative ways. Through a writing workshop facilitated by Tim Sheard, the students from the Essex County Consortium began to pour out their hearts from pen to paper, their thoughts and life experiences. They became confident about their writings. Publishing *Journeys Near and Far* gives our students validation that they are writers and they, too, have something to share.

Journeys Near and Far was made possible because Tamalois Axt, Dave Bass, Renae Brown, Rebecca Feit-Klein, Ellen Ray, Tim Sheard, and, of course, the students shared their time and talents.

Judith Celestin, Director,
Essex County College-Adult Learning Center

Henyetta Patrice Allen has been attending Fresh Start Academy for the past two years working toward my high school diploma. I love cooking. When I have completed my studies, I plan to study culinary arts.

Mom is Always With Me

Henyetta Patrice Allen

In the year of 1973, I, Henyetta Patrice Allen was born at Metropolitan Hospital in East Harlem, New York.   I was the ninth and the youngest child of Henry Lee All and Odessa Lee Young. My beautiful parents were both from the South, mom from West Virginia and dad from Orangeburg, South Carolina.

Raising nine children was not easy, but mom had enough love in her heart for an army. Born under the sign of Cancer, she was a very strong women who cared not only for her own family, but for those who were less fortunate. She was always giving to local charities or to the church. She loved helping her community in any way she could. She organized block parties for the neighborhood and put together trips in the summer for children in the community.

My mother was born with asthma. She never smoked a day in her life and took very good care of herself. Unfortunately, there were times she would get so sick from the asthma, my brothers would have to take her to the Emergency Room. The doctors would examine her and immediately they would have to intubate her. Listening to the nursing staff tell my mother to hold her breath while they shoved a tube down her throat into her chest so she could breathe was heart breaking.

As I grew older I began to really take notice of the

kind of woman my mother was. I was about eleven or twelve when my mom came home with tears in her eyes. My brothers and sisters gathered around her, hugging her and wiping the tears from her eyes. They kept asking, "Mama, what's wrong?" After a minute or two she began to tell us how she just lost her best friend, Miss Jean.

Miss Jean was like a sister to my mom and an auntie to us. Auntie Jean was a very beautiful woman. She was 5'4", light skinned, with freckles and auburn hair. She loved to dress in nice, neatly pressed clothes and matching shoes. Soon after her passing, mom took custody of two of Miss Jean's grandchildren. Mom raised them as her own. I was no longer the baby, they became my younger brother and sister. As time went on my older siblings moved out and it was just the three of us that mom had to care for.

In the next few years mom developed sugar diabetes and it really took a toll on her body, She lived many years with this disease, trying to never let it get her down. I was older now and had begun helping my mom with everything, from preparing meals to helping the kids with homework and transporting them back and forth to school. I attribute my passion for cooking to my mother. Cooking was one of the many gifts that mom passed on down to me. I love to cook and I am proud to say thanks to my mom for that great gift.

In the year 2000, my mom passed away. A month after her passing I gave birth to my first child, a beautiful baby boy. Although God called mom home to be with Him, He never left me alone. I was given a son to remind me of mom's beauty and the constant love that she gave to everyone she knew.

I know that mom always wanted me to go back to school to get my high school diploma. Today I am proud to say I am a student at the East Orange Adult Learning Program. My goal is to obtain my diploma and go on to attend Star Academy Culinary School. Before mom died I'd promised her I'd take care of the kids and always keep her love alive. It is a struggle, dealing with my own health issues, taking care of my own children, trying to get an education and still be there for my husband. Yet, I still wake up every day recalling my promise and mom's strength and love. Knowing mom is always with me gives me the strength I need to move mountains. I can do this!

Princess-Ann Allen is a student in the 1199SEIU Training and Employment Funds program in South Orange, NJ. She lives in Essex County. She is studying for her GED. Princess lives with her mom and four year old daughter who also goes to school. She is enjoying the lessons of the classroom and being a mom.

ZOO

Princess Allen

The animals

The people

Our lunch

Happy

My daughters having a nice time

It's our special time

2015-16

Toni Auerbach: I currently serve as Program Director of Fresh Start Academy ABE Program and have done so for the past 15 years. During the day, I teach grade school children. In my spare time, I enjoy boating, day trips with my husband and spending time with my 9 grandchildren.

A Door Closes, Another Opens

Toni Auerbach

I have worn many hats in my lifetime. Currently I'm a loving wife of 38 years; a devoted mother of three, married children; a grandmother of nine adorable grandchildren; a veteran teacher of 28 years; an Adult Ed. Program Coordinator in the evening, and a life-long, devout catholic. My life was filled with trials and tribulations, as with most of us. However, I am a firm believer that everything happens for a reason. My faith in God and his plans for me have kept me above water my whole life.

My journey with Adult Education began about fifteen years ago, primarily out of financial necessity. I had earned a Bachelor's Degree in Business, but had been working as a special needs teacher under emergency certification in a private school. Consequently my salary wasn't much to speak of, coming from someone with a degree. However, this was the exact place I needed to be while my children were still in school. The principal was understanding about my taking time off to tend to the needs of my children. This was certainly not my plan, but of course, GOD had a different plan.

I needed to make more money, and luckily, a friend of mine told me about a part-time evening position, teaching ESL students at Fairlawn Community

School in the evenings. This is where it all started.

I found teaching ESL students much more rewarding than teaching youth during the day. These students had a desire to learn and succeed in life. I loved hearing about life in their country and how they transitioned to America. The days were long, but I was earning extra money and enjoying what I did. A few years later that program ended, but fortunate for me, I had made a lifelong friend, and with the grace of GOD, one door closed, but yet another one opened.

This is the way life has always been for me. God has always put me where I needed to be when I needed to be there. My friend Pat found work for us at Bergen Community College also working with ESL students. Life was good; tiring but good.

I had long prayed for a position in a public school district, and this time a former colleague reached out to me and arranged an interview for me at a public school in Edgewater. The interview went well and I was hired on the spot. I was so elated. I was finally earning a decent salary.

Working in Edgewater was short lived. GOD must have known what a toll the commute and the long hours were taking on me. Once again, one door opened another closed. Attending my son's college soccer games, I became quite friendly with the coach's wife. She alerted me about an opportunity to pilot a program for inclusion at Essex County Vocational Tech. I wasn't looking for a job, but she insisted I meet with her boss. She, too, set up an interview for me and I reluctantly went. I was offered the job, a $15,000 raise and it was so much closer to home. It was a win, win situation, so I thought.

As an inclusion teacher I worked alongside many wonderful people. God put Finessa in my life. I worked with her during the day and discovered she was spear- heading a GED program in the evening at the Montclair Adult Learning Center, not far from where I lived in Verona. Finessa reached out to me to join her staff of teachers. At the Center I was preparing students to get a GED. GOD continues to walk with me on my journey toward success. Teaching in an urban High School is not a piece of cake. I'm earning more money now than I'd ever had, but some people refer to it as "combat pay".

One day a shooting took place on the front steps of the school. We were all on lock down. This now became a crime scene that I was a part of. So Scary! I'm safe. Life is still good......Untill!!!

Just as I approached the end of my third year teaching at the Voc. Tech I received the dreaded pink slip! I had no idea I was working and being paid under a grant program and that when the funding for the program was over so was the job. I was devastated. I went from making a nice salary to $0. I asked myself, "How would we live"? We would not be able to pay the mortgage on our newly purchased home on my husband's salary alone. To make matters worse, my mother was diagnosed with ovarian cancer and the doctors had given her less than five years to live. Just as I thought GOD had deserted me, once again, one door closed and another one opened.

Since I had no promise of employment in hand, I was able to collect unemployment for the summer. I emptied my mom's apartment and moved her in with me. I spent the summer praying for a job and tending to my mom, which once again was where I needed to be. My work ethics and professionalism had always left a lasting impression on those that I've worked with and for. People were reaching out to try and help me land a new position. Finessa was my guardian angel once again. She spoke with a former employer of hers in the East Orange School District. I met with the Director, Arlene King at the Bernie L. Edmunson Alternative High School. We spent quite a bit of time together and seemed to really connect. She, too, was a mother of three, an educator, and a minister of the church. She also started out as a business major just like me. This was ironic. She told me that someday she would retire and she would like to see me take over as the director of the adult education program. At the end of the interview she hired me. I was so happy you would have thought I'd won the lottery.

This was a twelve month position with a flexible teaching schedule. I was also able to use my business skills for data collecting and entering. I was able to get my mom to her doctor appointments, work and still make more money than with the previous job. I was so blessed, I thanked GOD daily for yet another great gift.

Three years later I had been named "Teacher of the Year" for my school building. My family and friends were so happy for me. This was a great job! Yet little did I know another setback was in the air.

Once again I needed one more day to become tenured when something bad happened. The state decided to remove Adult Education as a line item in the budget. This had a significant impact on our program. We were no longer 12 month employees. All of the tenured teachers were relocated and moved to other teaching positions. Those of us who were non-tenured received the dreaded pink slip. The program became just an evening grant program. I was still able to work in the evening, but there was no way I could afford to survive on an hourly part-time job. I was so upset again, but I decided to let go and let GOD handle this.

I collected unemployment for the summer and spent time taking care of mom. The cancer was getting worse. Little did I know this would be the last summer I would spend with her. I went on interviews, but my age and/or experience seemed to hamper me from getting the job. Districts could pay two teaching salaries for the one salary I was expecting to start at.

Finally, two weeks before school was to open I was offered an elementary school teaching position in the same district. "Thank you Jesus." My prayers had been answered. Ms. King also called me to arrange a meeting. She had wonderful news to share. She wanted to congratulate me on being named "East Orange's District Teacher of the Year." She also asked, "Do you remember what I told you when I first met you?" I said, "Of course I do? She told me that she was thinking of retiring at the end of the school year and that I should make sure I have all my credentials in place. By now, I had a Bachelor's in Business Administration, a post-bach degree in teaching, 33 credits in special ed, a Masters Degree in Curriculum, and a N.J. Supervisor's Certificate. But I didn't have a principal's certificate. Back to college I went. This meant more time away from mom and my family, but I had to do this. I prayed on it and once again with God's grace I earned my Principal's certificate. As sick as she was, my mom supported me every step of the way. Ms. King encouraged me and mentored me in the evenings. I tried to mirror her excellence. By the end of the year she had retired. On May 28th 2007, Mom passed away peacefully in the evening at our home. My East Orange family stood beside me as I put mom to rest.

As the Program Coordinator I have experienced many changes in The Adult Ed program. Each year offers a new set of challenges. I've seen my students come and go, fail and succeed. The clock keeps ticking, waiting for no one. One door closes and another opens. I am so grateful to be able to use the talents that GOD has blessed me with. THANK YOU GOD FOR NEVER LEAVING MY SIDE.

Helping People Help Themselves
Since 1939

Barry Batts was born and raised in Queens, New York City. Due to family neglect, I never had any formal schooling. At 55, I have struggled hard for the good place I am in life. I am currently working with my tutor to improve my reading and writing. You will understand more about me when you read my short memoir. It felt good to put it on paper.

Life Is Good To Me Now

Barry Batts

My name is Barry Batts. I want to tell you a story about my life and how I got to this point in my life. First of all, life is good for me now, but is wasn't always that way. Being born in the United States and being a child growing up you would hope to have good parents—a mommy and a daddy. But that was just a dream for me and my siblings. There were seven of us children born to my father and mother but there were seven others born to my mother by other men. Life for me was not easy growing up. When I was a little boy I remember looking at television shows in the 60s and how it showed loving families. But we never saw that in our family. Why couldn't we be like the families on TV? I remember my father was in the U.S. Army and he would come home on leave to spend time with his family. My siblings and I would try to dress in the best clothing we had at that time to impress dad. Little did my father know that we were hungry, we had not eaten for two days. I remember one Christmas Eve when my mother had beaten us and left us home for a few days alone in the house with no food while she went to her boyfriend's house. But when my mother knew my father was coming home she would beat him home and tell us kids to lie to him and tell him we were in school. It seemed like he believed us. We lived in my uncle's house but we had to sleep on a damp basement floor. My mother was getting public assistance to help take care of us and my dad was sending us an allotment check once a month to help take care of us. But my mother would give the checks to her boyfriend and we went without. I remember one morning we were so hungry my brother and I snuck upstairs as my sister looked out at the side door to see if anyone was coming. We snuck into the kitchen. We looked into the bottom cabinet as we slowly and cautiously opened the squeaking door. We looked and decided to take a can of corn from the back of the cabinet so it wouldn't be so obvious among the other canned goods. My brother ran downstairs with the can but I wasn't as fast. I got caught by my uncle and he told my mother on me. I tried to lie and say I went upstairs to see what time it was, even though I couldn't tell time. My mother beat me so bad and for some reason she was biting my hands like they were a piece of meat.

It seemed like I was always getting beaten for things, I never knew why. I remember one August evening when my grandmother came over to our house. We had just seen our father that day. She was very mad. She was screaming and cursing at me and I did not understand why. My mother grabbed me and she and my grandmother tore my clothes off me. There was an extension cord nearby and I hoped they wouldn't see it, but they did. Each time it hit my bare skin it burned. I thought they were enjoying it and the only reason they stopped was the neighbors banging on the front door threatening to call the cops because of my loud screams. My mother never registered me and three of my siblings for school, so that is why I never went to school as a child. To make the neighbors think we were in school my uncle would take us out in his car in the morning and over to his mother's house. Some of our neighbors began to wonder if we were in school. But sending us to my grandmother's house, where we would sit in her backyard all day, allowed us to stay hidden from the school authorities in New York City, one of the greatest cities in the United States. My mother lied to them and told the authorities that we had moved down south, and they believed her. So they never came looking for us after that. But it seemed like no one really cared. My father left us. I hoped he would have come back and taken us with him, maybe to his mother and father's house in North Carolina, but I guess that was wishful thinking. I had to grow up fast, starting with a paper route, raking leaves and shoveling snow around the neighborhood. When I got old enough, my first real job was cleaning a motel and working in factories. I had to grow up very fast in order to make sure my younger siblings would not suffer. They had to eat and have a clean bed to sleep in and clean clothes to go to school in. So I had to start quick, and it was worth it: My siblings were very successful. They made me proud. So we got something good out of a sad childhood upbringing when no one else cared and the authorities didn't look for us. My mother kept having different boyfriends but they always were married men. She kept getting pregnant, bringing more hungry mouths to feed. Then the men would leave and go back to their wives. It was bad enough for us but the babies had to eat and needed diapers. Mr. and Mrs. Robinson, who lived in one of the houses where I raked leaves on one of my routes, took a special liking to me. They were an elderly couple with no children, so they treated me like a son. They would give me an allowance for the chores I would do for them. As soon as I got it I ran to the supermarket and bought groceries, baby formula and diapers for the babies because their daddies would not. My mother gave her friends some of the children born out of wedlock, but the rest stayed with us. So you see why I had to work hard to do whatever I could. It made me a strong person. When I fall, with God's help I get back up. We were children living in a damp dark Laurelton, Queens basement: forgotten about. But my siblings and I did not become statistics in the penal system. I put my own interests aside to take care of my family and helped get them all off to a good start. Thank you, God, now I can concentrate on myself. I know that every child has the right to an education, but I missed out due to my mother. r. I somehow taught myself to read and write, at least enough to get by. Now I am studying with my tutor who volunteers to help. My goal is to someday get my GED. So in closing, everything my parents failed to do we did better. To my siblings: we are determined. To my parents: you tried to keep us down and hold us back: you lost!

Miranda Blackman is a student in the 1199SEIU Training and Employment Funds program in South Orange, NJ. She is a 38 year old female who migrated to the USA 7 years ago. The pride of her life is her almost ten year old son. She's a wife, mother and a Christian. Her ultimate goal is to become a pediatric nurse. She loves caring for people.

My Home

Miranda Blackman

Many family photos of smiling faces,
hanging on the walls

A lot of chatter and laughter along with good
music

Delicious foods being prepared and scented
candles everywhere

The macaroni and cheese along with the
barbecue chicken my husband made

The lawn in the front yard with my bare feet

An enormous amount of love and affection
for everyone

Each individual who enters my home is
welcome and loved.

Literacy Volunteers of America Essex & Passaic Counties

Beralia Briceno grew up in Honduras where she worked as a teacher in the Central American country. In the U.S. she developed an interest in the environment and earned an associate's degree from Utah Valley State College (now Utah Valley University) in Provo, with a specializwation in environmental science. In her spare time she enjoys riding bicycles with her 9-year-old daughter and reading books about water treatment.

My Free Life In Danli

Beralia Briceno

When I think about my early life in Danli, Honduras the word "free" comes to my mind. I remember flying kites, feeling the fresh air in my face, and running through the spacious fields. The sweet smelling wild flowers made me feel very close to nature. I loved the sound of the small ravine where I frequently swam. Sometimes I walked over the suspension bridge that swayed over the ravine. My mom was at home waiting for us to come for her dinner. We had delicious tortillas, with cheese, beans, rice and eggs. Our table was very crowded with five sisters and one brother and of course my dad who came home very tired from driving a tar truck to and from the city. At the weekend our whole family took care of our small field where we planted corn, beans, yucca and plantain. We kept some food for ourselves and the rest my father and brother would sell to the Mercado in town. We also helped our mother with some chores before going to school - like feeding the chickens and the pigs and gathering the eggs for breakfast. My brother helped to milk the three cows and to feed Lucero, our horse. Climbing in the trees was my favorite thing to do. I would find mangos, guavas, oranges and I would eat them while sitting in the tree with my sister Ana. We played rayuela (hopscotch) and hide and seek. It was difficult to find each other because there were many, many places to hide. After we did all our morning chores we were ready to go to school. It was a very long walk on rough roads but we played and sang many songs. It was fun and we were joined by other neighbors. Our teacher Matilde was a very nice and dynamic lady who taught grades 1-3. She recognized that I was a type of child who liked to ask questions and to get answers. We did not have a library so she brought many books for us to borrow. She advised us to study hard. Looking back I realize how wonderful my childhood was and how it helped me to be a good person and a caring mother. I am sorry that my daughter who lives in the city cannot climb trees, care for farm animals and run near sweet smelling fields as I did.

Ashley Brown is a student in the 1199SEIU Training and Employment Funds program in South Orange, NJ. She loves to try and do different things. She also loves to travel the world and see new things. She loves fashion and one day hopes to start her own clothing line. Ashley likes meeting new people. She loves her kids and she loves herself.

Florida

Ashley Brown

Beautiful palm trees

Different types of people

Beautiful beaches, amusement parks

Sounds of kids playing and having fun

Laughter and enjoyment on other people's faces

Fresh air, pine trees

Cleanness of the pool water

Foods like sushi, Indian, Chinese, even buffet foods

Water

Free, calm, wonderful

Peaceful, stress-free

It feels like my second home

I love going there three times a year with my
husband and kids

Denise Brown is a student in the 1199SEIU Training and Employment Funds program in South Orange, NJ. Denise lives in Irvington. She loves working with children. She likes planting and watching things grow.

Florida

Denise Brown

Beautiful trees, grass

The animals, the horses

The fresh air

Vegetables and fruit

My family, my friends

Happy

I love people, places and things

Albert Butler is a student in the 1199SEIU Training and Employment Funds program in South Orange, NJ. He was born and raised in Newark, NJ. His parents taught him many responsibilities, which made him the adult he is today. With his own family to guide now, he's found that there's no excuses in life. Now is the time to get back to school and take care of business.

My Job

Albert Butler

Kids kissing parents bye before jumping on the bus on their way to school

Kids on the back of the bus, filled with excitement about how fun school is going to be

Early morning snacks, eaten by kids before reaching school

My own early morning snacks to cover the growling of my stomach

All gadgets on the bus to make sure everything is operating safely to ensure the safety of the children

Myself as the driver, the biggest responsibility to make the children feel safe at all times

Maybe one day I'll own my own company and will forever change lives

Tammie Byrd is a mother, daughter, friend and an author. It took her a long time to get to where she is today. Although there were many setbacks and doubts, she was determined to hold on to her dreams. Pushing through tough times has made her who she is today and for that she is proud. She feels that this is just the beginning of her life's story and she has a lot to tell.

I Am An Author

Tammie Byrd

For as long as I can remember I have always been able to put words together and make a story. I could look at a picture, color, title, anything simple and my imagination would start working overtime. I would dig into my pocketbook and pull out my paper and pencil, quickly write it down so I would not forget. "What if..." "One day," I would say to myself.

My first try, I would cut out words from the newspaper and put them together. It didn't make sense to others, but it said a lot to me.

Next, I started writing short stories t pass my time. It became a hobby and a passion — something I couldn't let go of!

One day in class my teacher made an announcement: Essex Community College will be accepting submissions to showcase our writing talent. Bingo, here's my chance. I'm going for it.

I went home excited about what I'm going to write. A couple of hours later I wrote a rough draft and sent it to my teacher. She replied, "I like it!" She helped me put it together and bring it to life.

Once it was finished, I hit the send button. A couple of weeks later she made another announcement. The book of writings was finished and there was going to be a book signing. A big event.

Wow," I said. I couldn't stop smiling. I was hyped. I'm famous, now! My name in big letters, bright lights. There were decorations, balloons, pictures of the authors. It was truly a day I would never forget. In the end I was asked for my autograph. "I did it."

My first submission is now published in Connections Through Expressions currently on Amazon. "Why stop there?" I said to myself. I entered my submission in a writing contest, even though I didn't win, but it was good enough to be published in their magazine and will be coming out soon. Something so small turned into something big.

I'm on my way. Next, bigger letters, brighter lights.
Tammie Byrd

Estatelis Camps

A Big Surprise

Estatelis Camps

My son is seven years old. His name is Michael. He is a happy boy, and he is always smiling. He has blond, curly hair, and his eyes are green. Everyone loves him so much. People tell me all the time how lovely he is, at the school and in his program, and all of my family. He is so smart, too.

About two months ago I went to the M&M store in New York City to buy an Easter present for him; I went with a friend. I bought two cups, a blanket, a pillow and a backpack. He didn't go with me because it was a surprise.

When he came home from his grandparents' house, I said, "Papi, come see what I have for you."

Then I gave him the present. He sat on the sofa, and it was amazing to see the expression on his face. He was very surprised, because he wasn't expecting a present from that store and he loves that store; he was smiling so much during those first two minutes that he couldn't open the gift.

When he finally decided to unwrap it, he took his time to enjoy each item, one by one, looking at the cups, touching the blanket and the pillow and trying on the backpack.

Then he said, "Thank you so much for the present, mommy! I love it!"

Oh my God! My heart felt very excited. Michael does not know that I received a gift that day just as precious. I felt so much joy seeing my boy so happy.

Theresa Charlery

Fishing in Micoud, St. Lucia

Theresa Charlery

My Name is Theresa Charley. I was, born in the fishing village of Micoud on the South-East Coast of St. Lucia. My parents are Peter and Genovefa Promesse. I have two sisters and five brothers. I am the second oldest of my parents' children's. I also have half-siblings. Back then, the same men in the Caribbean would always meet other women and create another family. It was always good whenever my siblings came home for the holidays, we used to have lots of fun.

Growing up at school, there were what we called hard bullies. They would always eat my lunch. My mother would buy one pound of chicken for the family to share. I would always have to fight in school because the bullies would eat my lunch. My sister would tell on me that I was fighting and my mother would then beat me. The very next day, I would get into a fight again, and then get a beating for fighting. My dad would say to my mother, "Genovefa stop beating the child. She will do it any way." Finally, my sister told my mother that children were eating my lunch, so she stopped beating me and I stopped fighting.

On Saturdays my mother, two sisters and I would go by the river to wash clothes. I would always leave the clothes with my sister to wash and go with my brothers to fish. We would catch a lot of fish! Oh, yes, I would have lots of fish on my plate. My parents were farmers. We had bananas, plantain, yellow yam, dasheen, sweet potatoes. We never went hungry for food, but we never had a lot of meat on our plates. My parents did not have a lot of money. She would buy one pound of meat for everybody to share in the household.

I made promise to myself and God that I would never have so many children. If I ever had a child, I would always want the best for my child. God blessed me with a beautiful little girl. I named her Tannel. I never laid a hand on her skin, I loved her so much. She means the world to me.

While she was growing up, we would eat a whole chicken, just for the two of us. I was happy my daughter became an Accountant, no more going without meat. Although I became a vegetarian, once in the while I still think about the chicken my mother used to cook. She is a very good cook.

Marie Confident is a student at Essex County College. She is learning English because she wants to be a nurse in the United States. She wants to help people who need food and medical care.

God Is Able

Marie Confident
Essex County College

My name is Marie Confident, I have three beautiful children. The oldest is 20 years old, the second is 11 years and the third is 6 years old. I have two girls and one son. I had a hard time with my son because he can't read and write, but little by little he's getting better because I believe in God. God can do anything he chooses because he's the creator. I try to hear the advice that some people are giving me because you are never too old to take any advice. I'm a strong Haitian woman and I believe in myself. My mother has been in the United States for about 17 years now. She was the one who applied for us to come to the United States. Now we have about 6 years in the U.S. It was 12 of us who came to the United States. I was in my country working as an R.N. I was working with Portor without Border, and as well as University Hospital at Port-au-Prince. I loved my job because I was able to touch people that were sick and it was really hard for them; but I felt their pain. Now I'm working as a home health aide because I love taking care of people. I'm working for an agency for 3 years. It's not easy for me sometimes because I have to take care of my kids, go to school, then go to work to pay my bills, because I'm struggling on my own and the only person I have is God.

It's not easy working in the Nursing field because you don't have enough time to even eat something because you're helping people and sometimes the odors aren't even good for your system. My husband is still in my country right now and I'm currently waiting for immigration to give him his papers to come to the United States. Once he comes, he will help me out a lot. Then I will have time to study and start back again as an R.N. because that's my goal and that's what I want to accomplish. I know I can do it because I believe in God and I believe in myself. My older daughter is in college. She is in the nursing school at Essex County. Her name is Margastalie Montina. When she's in her 4th year of college, she will be a lot of help to me because I'm getting old and we have to move on. But with God nothing is impossible. My goal is to be done taking the test and to pursue my dream to pass my nursing exam. I would like for my daughter and me to be working at the same agency.

Fernanda Contreras was born in Calarcá, an important coffee producing municipality in eastern Colombia. She earned a bachelor's degree in eco-business and worked in her country's burgeoning eco-tourism industry before coming to the U.S. She is married and has a 12-year-old daughter, to whom she wrote her prize-winning poem as a letter. She's an avid English student who enjoys teaching Spanish to tutors in LVA's English-Spanish Language Exchange, which she helped launch. When she's not studying English, Fernanda enjoys exercising outdoors, bicycling with her husband, and taking aerobics and zumba classes.

A Christmas Letter

Fernanda Contreras

Dear darling daughter, It's Christmas and it's a very special day. The people are very happy. They eat turkey and ham, and drink wine. Also, they sing songs around the Christmas tree. The children leave cookies and milk for Santa Claus. When they wake up, they open their gifts. But in Colombia, it's different. During the week before Christmas day, the children pray around the nativity and sing typical songs like: Nana, The River Fishes, and Go Pastors Go. Then people eat natilla with bunuelos, and lechona. When it's 12 PM on Christmas Eve, the children open the gifts. The adults dance and drink beers while the children play with their new toys. I know for 6 years I have not seen you, but I remember your face, your hands, your smile, and scent. You are always on my mind and in my heart every day of the year. Please don't forget I love you and you are my gift from God. I hope you will go far in your life. You can touch the stars and make your dreams come true. It does not matter what you choose. If you want to be a doctor, nurse of teacher, I will be happy. What I will always look for is your happiness. If you want to see me, you can see the moon because we are under the same moon. If you want to feel me, you can feel your heart. If you want to kiss me, I send my kisses in the wind. I promise darling daughter, your heart and my heart are one beat. Merry Christmas my angel.

Your mother

Juana Fernandez was born in Dominican Republic. I belong to a big family; so I am the number ten of twelve siblings. My life was hard, so I grew up without my father, because he died when I was very little. My mother and older brothers educated me. Over the years I have been preparing; always thinking about being on the top despite the adversity; fighting to get the best of myself. I graduated from high school in my country in 1994, with very good score. At that time I knew that I should be able to follow my dreams; and continued working in different areas of works. Years later I applied for a scholarship to study in the university. in 2003, I finally, became an Ophthalmic Technician from the Pedro Henriquez Urena University and Dr. Elias Santana Hospital; that happened in my country also. For four years, I worked as an Optometrist, in Lopez Optical. Part of my duties were: training contact lens and work with visual plan. I got married in 2008. Two years later moved with my husband to US (Newark, NJ) to begin a new life. Since I arrived in this country my first goal was to learn English. That's why I took classes in different schools, until I graduated from ESL Adult Learning Center, Essex County College in 2016. Right now I am working as Home Aide. But in this year, just in 2017, I am planning to increase my English skills and becoming a US citizen, as well as to validate my certification from my country. In addition with this step I will have the opportunity to work in the professional area that I like!

My Sick Nephew

Juana Fernandez

It was at the beginning of spring, in March of 2014, exactly two years ago. At that time, everything seemed perfect in my life and my family's life, too. Then I placed a call to my sister's house. It was a Friday morning. The phone rang, rang and rang. I tried several times in the first 30 minutes, and I continued calling her until her husband answered the phone.

He said, "Hello, how are you?"

I said, "I'm ok. How about you?"

He answered, "Your sister is right now in the hospital."

I got nervous and asked him, "What has been happening?"

He told me, "Our older son Emmanuel is very sick. He has been in the hospital for three days, and he is still there! He is not getting better! We don't know what type of illness he has, and we don't know what we can do."

I told him that I wanted to call my sister, and he gave me the phone number where I could reach her. One hour later, I reached my sister on the phone, and we talked for a long time. I asked her, "What is happening?"

She cried! I could feel her sadness, and like her, I was very sad. So I gathered spiritual strength, and I said to her, "Ask the doctor, the nurse, ask anyone in the hospital: 'Have there been lab tests?'"

She said, "The doctor has not come in the whole day."

And I said to her, "Listen, you have to make a decision right now. Remember, it is your son's life. This is not a game! If they don't have any satisfactory answers for you right now, you have to request information about this illness and take your son elsewhere. You know that he is not getting better. Please! This is your son!" Before we finished the call, I added: "My sister, you know that I love you, and I want the best for you!"

Two hours later my sister was in another hospital with her son. My nephew was in intensive care in a children's hospital due to a coma. He was diagnosed with kidney failure due to dehydration through vomiting and diarrhea. My nephew stayed in the hospital for almost a month, receiving dialysis and a long treatment. Finally, the doctor let him go home with his family.

All the family was happy and all our friends were, too. My sister's community's church was praying all the time while my nephew was in the hospital. Three days later, my sister and all the family went to the church to participate in the Holy Mass and to say thanks to God for returning back to us our Emmanuel and for saving him.

The minister said, "Brother and sisters, thanks for your prayers! The child who we were praying for is here among us."

The minister put his book aside and said, "Emmanuel, come here in front us!"

That was a great moment! Everybody was surprised, crying and clapping for a longtime. Why? Because a lot of them were praying for a child, but they did not know it was Emmanuel, and that the child was my sister's son. It was a day of great rejoicing!

Monique Florestal was born in Saint-Marc, Haiti. She came to the United States in 1998 for a visit and decided that she wanted to make the U.S. her home permanently in 2000. She is a student in the 1199SEIU Training and Employment Funds program in South Orange, NJ were she is studying to get her high school diploma. She currently works in the medical filed and would like to become a LPN.

Dreams of a Child

Monique B. Florestal

There was a time when I was a little girl, I always dreamed of becoming a nurse, and then a lawyer. Suddenly everything changed.

I remember when I was dreaming of becoming a nurse, I would always act like a nurse. It was as if I already was one. For example, I used to have a pretty doll named Dinah, and she was my patient. I had to listen to her heart, take her blood pressure, and even give her medication. Dinah was always sick. Day and night I'd have to take care of her. She would even sleep with me so I could keep an eye on her.

But by the time I got to high school, everything changed. My dream of being a nurse disappeared. I wanted to be a lawyer, but that did not go far. Instead, I started taking classes to become an engineer. However, when I came here to the U.S., I had to study to get my high school diploma, for which 1199 helped me to study. Now I am thinking of training to be an LPN after taking my H.S. diploma. And with that I can really be the nurse I was dreaming of. I can take care of real people, like I used to do for little Dinah. My love for Dinah for all those years helped me to pursue my dream to become a nurse.

Anka P. Forrest

Daniel's Decision

Anka P. Forrest

Michael got up earlier than usual that morning. This was the day of his son's arrival to the United States. He was worried about his son Daniel because it was a long time since they talked about buying a new house. Though Michel did not want to say anything to Daniel for the past six months, he could not stop thinking about it. Daniel decided to take the time off this year and spend his spring break with the family. Myra, Daniel's mother, was coming with Daniel's wife Ivana, and the two small children, Dimitri and Peter. Their plane was scheduled to land at the Newark Airport at noon. The sound of Michael's phone woke me up from deep sleep. The loud speaker was on.

"Dad!" Daniel's voice sounded agitated. "Don't forget to get diapers on your way, salmon and lettuce. Ivana wants to fry salmon today. Don't be late this time, please!"

"Yes, son. " Michael responded. "Relax. Everything will be fine. How are the babies?"

"Dimitri was fussing a lot. We left his favorite toy at home, and he wanted no other. That reminds me to tell you, get another beanie that looks like a bee. He likes those. Peter slept through the whole trip. We can't wait to see you."

Michael sighed. He remembered how Daniel sounded when he was a little boy. The children's voices in the background mixed with the sounds of Myra's voice as she made another futile attempt to keep them quiet.

"Oh, by the way, did you leave yet?" Daniel said in a commanding tone.

"I am about to in a minute. Got to grab my camera." Then the door slammed.

There wasn't much traffic on the way to the mall, so Michael had plenty of time to take care of things on his way there. Daniel's sister Saniya arrived with her daughter Emily early to beat the traffic. She knew that Emily was going to ask for pizza, so they left home early to have time for stopping at Domino's. Saniya, too, was worried about Daniel, but for a different reason. She knew nothing about Michael's and Daniel's plan, but dreaded hearing their arguments. Michael kept this from her to avoid the kind of confrontations they have had in the past.

The plane was on time. Emily grew more impatient to go home and watch cartoons. She was in no mood to stay there a minute longer. They left the airport while Michael and Daniel still waited for the luggage. Daniel looked at his father in anticipation. They said nothing to each other for perhaps half an hour. Michael was rewinding the last conversation they had a decade ago. That was how long ago it was. To Daniel, Michael father looked not much older, but more withdrawn. He wasn't used to his father being any different than at that time when they really discussed things. This was bothering Daniel because Michael was always the one to break the silence first.

Though Michael could not stop thinking about that last conversation he had with his son, he resolved to leave it all in God's hands. While Daniel had agreed with him on buying a home in a quieter place, he did nothing on his part afterwards. It was bothering Michael. At that moment, Michael wondered whether he could trust himself with handling another dialog with Daniel. This time the silence was too unbearable for Daniel.

"Dad! What's wrong?"

"Nothing."

Seriously! What's wrong, are you mad at me for something? Sorry I was a little abrasive on the phone this morning."

Michael looked at his son. Daniel looked just like Myra with that guilty expression on his face. Like Myra, Daniel has an oval face, straight dark brown hair and dark brown eyes. Much taller than Michael, Daniel could see that much of his father's hair was turning white. There were still reasons to fear the possible outcome of this conversation, but Michael suddenly felt the urge to answer.

"No, son. I wanted to ask you something, but you have to promise me that this time you won't get mad at me like you usually do. I was afraid to say anything to you because you were always too busy to talk. I didn't want to bother you. Since you haven't said anything about your plans for almost a year..." Michael expected to be interrupted by Daniel. He was.

"What plans? You've lost me, Dad!"

"Never mind," sighed Michael. "You're tired from the trip. We can talk about it some other time, after you get more rest."

"What do you mean *never mind?*"

"Just that. I don't want to upset you again. It's okay if you don't want to discuss it."

"Discuss what, MICHAEL?" Daniel's voice was getting louder.

"Here we go again...you need to calm down. Anger is not good for your heart and you know that heart disease runs in our family. Maybe, it's not worth the risk."

"Oh. Sorry, Dad. About that house near the newly build Valero gas station. Listen. None of these places have acceptable living conditions. The buildings I looked at are cheap, but they have to be torn down. They were condemned by the public service due to bad electrical installations and problems with sewage. There is no running water. The contractor who built the place never had the approval from the state. As it is now, the state has confiscated the property because it does not meet the safety standards. People were dumping used oil in the river so the air smells so bad it's hard to breathe."

"Daniel, if you only told me anything about this earlier..."

"I know Dad. I'm so sorry."

"It's okay, son. I understand this isn't working out, but we still have to keep trying, right? Did you think about any other options?

"Wow! Dad! Your hands are like sand paper...why is the nail missing on your thumb?"

"It happened at work, son. See, I don't want this to happen to your children. This is why I wanted you to move out of the city. Schools in suburbs are so much better. You have an education so that you don't have to suffer through life like this. I hope that you want the same for your children, son."

"Do you have to work so much?" Daniel asked tearfully.

"You will understand, son, when your children get

older. You and your sister are all I have in this world. I care about you and I want to help you get out of that place. We have to find a better place for your family before Dimitri and Peter start school. I know you want the best education for your children. My opinion, if it means anything to you, is that we should keep looking."

"I am okay where I am. You don't have to worry, I have been considering other options. Something turned up back in February last year, but Mom told me not to mention anything to you until I see you," Daniel confessed.

Michael felt a sudden surge of anger. He remembered that Daniel often changed his mind under Myra's influence. This time, as he thought, was going to be no different.

"Why is your mother always meddling? WHY?"

"She's not! You don't understand. We talked about the new house and we both agreed that maybe this is not the right time. There's too much political turmoil in the country. People are only buying houses in Belgrade and its suburbs to rent them or to settle in when they retire. Not too many people from my generation venture into this sort of thing unless they make over a hundred thousand euros a year. They don't want to lose their investments to the state's greedy, corrupt politicians."

"Let me understand, son, are you just going to give up? Are you?"

"No, Dad, far from it. Mom found this old restaurant downtown. No one has bothered with it for almost twelve years. People don't have any money to start businesses in Serbia unless they live abroad. The

63

owner of the place went bankrupt. He wants me to take over the place before the state sends people to tear it down. I need you to co-sign as another owner of the place so that we can get the ownership license from the state, tear it down and build a café. You can bring your construction crew there. We can have our new apartment on the second floor. The kids can walk to school. Everything is close."

"How much is this going to cost?"

"Dad, trust me! It will cost much less than the new house in the suburbs. My old school friend has a law firm and it will be easy to get the state license. Mom is doing all the paperwork. She spoke to the owner and found out he's moving back to France to take care of his aging parents. A new mall is being built downtown and will be finished probably at the same time we open the café. Just trust me, Dad! Once the business takes off, we can buy the house anywhere and owe no debt!"

Michael looked into Daniel's face wondering what was really on his mind. It occurred to him that Daniel was doing this for Ivana. She could not imagine living farther than ten minutes away from the mall. Her father wanted her to live in the big city.

"Son, I just hope you know what you're doing." Michael said with resignation. "Whatever you decide, I am your father, I will support you one-hundred percent."

Danielle Grant is a student in the 1199SEIU Training and Employment Funds program in South Orange, NJ. She is from a beautiful, small island called Jamaica. She enjoys cooking and spending time with her family. Danielle works two jobs and attends school at the same time. She really wants to become a registered nurse because she loves taking care of people.

The Beach

Danielle Grant

Beautiful, blue sea water

Children screaming

Saltiness

Rough sand

At peace

Everyone having fun

It makes me so happy

Dejan Grier is a student in the 1199SEIU Training and Employment Funds program in South Orange, NJ. He lives in Irvington, NJ. Dejan wants to be a football player.

Home

Dejan Grier

The door to my room

My song playing

Home-cooked food

My game

Safe and loved

It's always going to be home for me

Maria Guallpa is a student in the 1199SEIU Training and Employment Funds program in South Orange, NJ. Maria lives in West Orange, NJ, with her family of 3 daughters and 1 son. She is from Ecuador. She works as a housecleaner.

The Forest

Maria T. Guallpa

Trees and birds

The sound of birdsong

Perfume of the flowers

Blueberries in the forest

Different plants and flowers

So wonderful

A place to relax and have more energy

Clifford Henry has spent more than 35 years in the Army Reserve, serving in Iraq and Guantanamo Bay, Cuba, among other military outposts. He has five children, the youngest a 17-year-old son, and works as a restaurant cook. As a teenager growing up in Florida, Clifford dropped out of school in order to work full-time. He came to LVA Essex & Passaic Counties in the hopes of earning a GED and, eventually, attending college. He said he won't quit his studies until these are done.

Confused Young Man

Clifford Henry

A young man was missing for three days. The mother and father were worried about their son.

The family put up photographs all over town. Along with the picture was the message: "If anyone has seen our son, call us."

The father called the police station.

Officer Reed said, "May I help you, please?"

The father said, "My son has been missing for three days."

Officer Reed said, "Someone will be over to take your report. What is your address?"

The father said, "222 Hillside Avenue."

His wife asked, "What did the police say?"

"They will be over in a half hour to take a report."

The doorbell rang. The father answered the door.

Officer Peterson said, "I'm here to take a report for a missing son."

The father said, "Come on in and have a seat."

Officer Peterson said, "Start from the beginning."

The father said, "Me and my son got into a big argument."

Officer Peterson asked, "About what?"

"He was stealing from us and would lie. He ran out the house. I ain't seen him since. I should have made it clearer before he went out the door."

Officer Peterson asked, "How old is your son?"

The father said, "Eighteen years old, and his name is Michael."

Office Peterson said, "We'll be in touch."

The father said, "Thank you very much, Officer Peterson."

The mother said, "Go up to his room and find some telephone numbers to call some friends."

The father was driving around in the neighborhood to find his son. He stopped at a couple of places he thought his son hung out at. He approached the young men on the corner. A young man said, "I saw him walking around on the streets. He was wearing blue jeans and a blue jacket."

The father said, "Thank you for your information."

He went back into the house. The mother called a couple of places — no answer. The father told his daughters that their brother was missing. The mother noticed some of his clothes were missing. The two daughters came over to the house. One daughter asked, "How long has he been missing?"

The father said, "At least three days. I didn't mean for him to leave."

The younger daughter asked, "Did you call any of his friends? He will come back when he cools down."

The other daughter asked, "What are you talking about, Dad?"

The father said, "Money was missing from the house. He wouldn't go to school. I got tired of it."

The father got a strange telephone call. A man said,

"If you want your son back, I want you to give me $3,000. I'll call tomorrow to tell you where to come. If you tell anyone, I will kill your son."

The father kept the phone call from his family. He did not want them to know.

The mother asked, "Who was that on the phone?"

The father responded, "It's no one, honey. I'll be right back."

The father went to the police station. He went up to the desk. "My son was kidnapped."

The police officer said, "Calm down, sir, take a deep breath. How do you know your son was kidnapped?"

The father said, "I got a phone call at my house from a man. He told me my son was kidnapped. I'm supposed to meet him tomorrow with $3,000. When I get more information, I will tell you."

The police officer said, "Go back home and wait until tomorrow. We will be there. Don't tell anyone."

The father went back to the house. He walked into the house. He did not say anything to anyone.

The wife asked, "Where did you go?"

He said, "I went to the police station."

She asked, "Why would you go to the police station?"

He said, "I got a phone call from someone to tell me our son was kidnapped."

The mother asked, "Why couldn't you tell me the truth about where you were going?"

He said, "I did not want to get the family upset. We all have to focus on the situation. The police officer is supposed to be here."

The police came to the house. The father asked, "What took you so long to get here?"

The officer said, "We had to put someone on the case."

The phone rang. The father picked up the phone. The police officer was recording the information. The man said, "Bring the money to 362 Drive Street, and make sure the money is in small bills. Make sure you come alone. If you love your son, you will do the right thing."

"How do I know my son is alive? Can I speak to him?"

The man said, "No more questions."

The father asked the officer, "Did you get all of that?"

The police officer said, "Yes, I'm going to replay the tape. Make sure we get everything we need on tape so we have this plan tight. Do you have the money?"

The father said, "Yes, I have the money. The money is put away."

The police officer said, "Go get the money and meet me outside."

The father said, "I'm very nervous."

The police officer said, "This is not the time to be nervous. You've got to be tough to get your son back. I will be following you. Don't give him any idea someone is following you. First, before you give him any money, make sure you see your son. Be very careful what you say to him. We've got police around the area."

The father spotted the man with his son.

The man asked, "You have the money?"

The father said, "Let my son go. I will give you the money."

The man said, "Give me the money and I give you your son, no trick."

The father threw the money over to the man. The son ran over to his father. The man ran away with the money. The police officers chased the man for a minute. The man ran into an abandoned house. The police officers surrounded the house. They said, "Come out with your hands up." The man was shooting at the police. The police officers shot back at the man. The man kept shooting. The police officers kept shooting back. The shooting stopped on both sides. The police officers rushed into the abandoned house. The police found the man dead on the floor. The man hid the money before he died. The police officers searched the house. They found the money under a board in the floor.

The report said, "The man is dead." The police went back to the location where the father and the son were standing.

The father asked, "Did you catch the kidnapper?"

The police officer said, "Yes, but the kidnapper is dead."

The father asked, "Did he have the money on him?"

The police officer asked the son, "Did you know the kidnapper?"

The young man said, "No"

The police said, "I have to take your son in for more information."

The father asked, "Can I take my son home now?" He demanded, "Where is my money? I'm not leaving till I get my money."

The police officer said, "The money is yours. Make sure your son will be there tomorrow morning."

The father said, "I will make sure he is there tomorrow morning."

The father said to his son, "Everyone will be glad to see you come home. Mother will be so happy to see you."

The father and son walked into the house. "The man was caught by the police officer. He was killed by the police officer."

The mother said, "Thank God my son is O.K. Did you get the money back from the police officer?"

The father said, "Yes, I got the money back. Count all the money. We both have to have a long talk about rules and regulations in this house. You have to listen to me and your mom. Go to school or to work. Do you have anything to say?"

The son said, "Mom and Dad, I will change. I'm so sorry for what I put you through, but I have a drug problem. I need help."

The father said, "We will get you help."

The mother said, "We love you very much. We want you to do right thing."

The father said, "Since we cleared all this up, everything is O.K. Let's go to the police station to clear everything. I will drive you there."

The son said, "Dad, I have something to tell you. Promise me you won't get mad at me, Dad."

The dad said, "I promise you I won't get mad at you. What's important, son, is to talk to me." He pulled the car over. "Tell me what you have to say."

"I planned the kidnapping, Dad. I made the call. The man was homeless on the streets. I knew he had a criminal record in the past. I told him he would get a thousand dollars. Only thing he needed to do was to go to the location and pick up the money. The man had no idea what was going on. I really need that money. I got in really big trouble with a drug dealer. I didn't have no idea where to get the money from. He will kill me in four days. I'm very sorry, Dad. I didn't want no one to get hurt. If the drug dealers can get to me, they will hurt my family. I do not know what to do."

The father said, "You got an innocent man killed for nothing. There's nothing I can do for you. Turn yourself into the police."

The son said, "Before I turn myself in, I will kill myself."

The father said, "Son, you do not have to kill yourself. Turn yourself in to the police. It will break your mother's heart if you kill yourself. Killing yourself won't solve the problem. Think for a minute before you go in. We will keep it to ourselves what we talked about. Promise me this will not happen again. I put my neck out for you, son, and you really have to keep what we talked about to yourself. Don't talk to no one about what you told me."

The son said, "Promise, Dad, I will keep that to myself. Thank you, Dad."

The boy walked into the police station and told the police that the man kidnapped him.

The policeman asked, "Did you know the man?"

The boy said, "I never saw him before."

The police officer said, "I'm going to ask you one more time, did you ever see this man before? If I find out you lied to us we're going to lock you up."

The boy said, "I am telling you the truth."

The police officer said, "You can leave, but we will be looking out."

The boy walked out of the police station. "That was very close," he thought.

The boy went back to the car. The father asked, "What did they say to you?"

The boy said, "I told the police that I did not know the kidnapper. If they find out I am lying, I am going to jail. Dad, I am very nervous and scared. I am going to have a drug dealer on my case soon. Dad, what should I do?"

The father asked, "You want me to give you advice? What should you do? Make a better life for yourself and go back to school. Stop putting this family in so much stress. How can I help you if you keep lying to me? I need to trust you. First, you need to prove to me you are a better person, which you have to become. I want to help you this time. I'm going to give you a second chance. Don't mention this to anyone, especially your mother."

The son said, "Thank you, Dad. I won't let you down, Dad."

The father said, "Let's go home."

They went home. The mother asked, "Was everything O.K. at the police station?"

The father said, "Everything is fine."

The mother said, "You must be really, really hungry."

The father said, "Don't forget what we talked about. Don't mention anything to your mother."

The son said, "Dad, I remember everything we talked about."

There was a knock at the door. The father answered the door. He asked, "May I help you?"

The drug dealer asked, "Can I speak to Pete?"

The father said, "No one here named Pete. Maybe you got the wrong house."

The drug dealer was searching for the house in the neighborhood.

The mother asked, "Who was that at the door?"

The father said, "Someone was looking for Pete. Do you know anyone named Pete?"

The son said, "Dad, That's the name I gave him. Did he say what he wanted? He's gonna keep searching until he finds me. He wasn't sure where I live."

The father said, "Lay low in the house for a couple days."

The son said, "Dad, he's not gonna stop until he finds me. I don't want to put this family in danger."

The mother came into the room. She asked, "What are you talking about? Don't lie to me. I need to know what you are talking about."

The father said, "Nothing."

The son wrote a note, "Mom and Dad, I love you both. Dad, thank you for everything you have done for me. This is the best thing for me to do — run away. I did not want to bring any trouble to my family."

The boy left the house. As he was walking, someone was following him. He kept looking back. A car got closer and closer. The boy started to run. The car approached him. The drug dealer said, "Get in the car." The boy kept running. The drug dealer stopped the car, got out and started running after the boy. The drug dealer caught up with him and beat him up. He drove away. A neighbor called the police. The police arrived at the scene. The boy was beaten very badly. The police called an ambulance. The ambulance came. The boy was rushed to the hospital. The police took a statement from the neighbor who had called the police. The lady said, "I saw a man beating up the boy."

The policeman asked, "Can you recognize the car he was driving?"

The lady said, "A black Mercedes."

The police officer said, "Thank you for the information you gave me."

He went to the hospital. "How bad is he?" he asked

the doctor. The doctor said, "He is in a coma and has a broken nose. You need to call a family member."

The police officer said, "He did not have any information on him. I will have another police officer sit by the door. Someone beat him up very badly. Do you recognize him?"

The other police officer said, "Yes, it was a case that happened a couple of days ago. We have to open this file and see where he lives. Don't leave this room. I will be back."

The first police officer found the file and went over to the boy's house. He rang the bell. The father answered the door. "Good afternoon, sir. My name is Officer Tony. Sir, do you recognize this picture?"

The father said, "Yes, that's my son. What happened?"

The mother asked, "Who's at the door?"

The father said, "The police."

Officer Tony said, "Your son was beaten up very badly."

The father asked, "Where is my son now?"

Officer Tony said, "He's at the hospital."

The mother and father drove to the hospital. They both went upstairs. They approached the nurse. The nurse said, "May I help you."

The father said, "Yes, ma'am. My son was beaten up. Can I see him?"

The nurse said, "Yes, Room 16."

They both went into the room. They started crying when they saw their son lying there.

The nurse said, "Your son is in a coma."

The mother asked the father, "Where are you going?"

"I am going to make a phone call." He called his daughter. He said, "Your brother was beaten badly. Call your sister."

His daughter asked, "Where is Mom?"

"She is sitting by his bedside."

The daughter said, "I will see you later, Dad."

He said, "Don't forget to call your sister."

He went back into the room. He said, "Carol will be here later. Tracy should be here soon."

The police officer came into the room. The mother asked, "Did you catch the person who did this to my son?"

He said, "I need to ask you a question about your son. Do you know who did this to your son?"

The father said, "I remember his face. He came to my house looking for my son."

The police asked, "Can I take you down to the police station to show you some pictures?"

The father said, "No problem."

He said to his wife, "Honey, I will be back. I'm going to the police station to look at some pictures."

The mother said, "Ok. Don't be long."

The police drove the father down to the station. The father was looking through the photos. The policeman asked, "Like to have some coffee?"

The father said, "Yes."

The police asked, "How you like it?" He brought the

coffee to the father.

The father looked at the pictures. He recognized the drug dealer's face in the photo book.

The police officer said, "Thank you very much. You did enough here."

The father went back to the hospital. His son was still in a coma. Tracy was in the room.

The mother said, "Did they have any luck catching the person?"

The father said, "No, they have a picture of the person. Go home and get some rest, honey. I will stay with him. I will call you if there are any changes. Tracy, take your mother home. Ain't much we can do here."

The daughter said, "Dad, I will be back. Do you want me to bring you something to eat?"

The father said, "Yes, make sure your mother eats."

Detective Mitchell came to the hospital. "I have good news. We caught the person. How's your son doing?"

The father said, "He's doing about the same."

Detective Mitchell said, "If there are any changes, give me a call."

The doctor came into the room. "Your son has swelling to the brain."

The father asked, "What does that mean?"

The doctor said, "We have to get the swelling down. If we get the swelling down, I think he will come out of the coma. Pray the swelling goes down."

The father called home. The phone rang three

times. The wife answered the phone. "Honey, I've got good news. They caught the person who beat up our son. The doctor said if the swelling goes down, he will come out of the coma. I will call you again if there are any changes."

The nurse came into the room and took another X-ray. She asked, "Would you like something to drink?"

He said, "Thank you very much."

The nurse came into the room with the drink. He said, "Thank you a lot."

The mother came back to the hospital with her daughters. The father asked the mother, "What are you doing here? You didn't have to come. I would have called you if there was any changes."

The mother said, "I couldn't sit home knowing my son is in the hospital."

He said, "The nurse came to the room and took X-rays. The doctor said if the swelling goes down, he will come out of the coma."

The mother said, "Let's pray he will come out of the coma."

The doctor came back into the room. "I have good news. The swelling went down. Let's keep our fingers crossed."

The father said, "The only thing we can do is wait and keep praying. Let's take a walk, honey, I have something to tell you. The drug dealer beat him up, because he owed him some money. The man who came to the house that day was looking for our son."

The wife asked, "Why didn't you tell me the truth the first time?"

He said, "You know I didn't want to get you upset. You have health problems. I didn't want to get you upset again. I got more to tell you. I will tell you it another time. Let's go back into the room. Don't mention it to anyone."

One daughter said, "Mom and Dad, he moved a little bit!"

The wife said, "Go get the nurse."

The nurse said, "May I help you, sir."

"My son is moving his hands."

The nurse and father rushed into the room. The son came out of the coma! Everyone was very happy. The nurse went to get the doctor. The doctor came back to the room. He asked the boy, "How are you feeling?"

The boy said, "I feel great. Why is everybody here?"

The doctor said, "You were in a coma for three days. You know everybody in this room?"

The boy said, "Yes."

The doctor said, "I need to keep him one more day to run more tests on him before I can release him. I want to make sure you are O.K."

The mother said, "Thank God you are O.K."

The nurse said to the boy, "You must be very hungry. I will bring you something to eat."

The boy said, "I thank everyone for being here."

The father said to the daughters, "Take your mother home. Everything will be all right here. I will be home later."

The mother said to the son, "I love you. I will see you later."

The father asked, "How are you really feeling today? The doctor will take the bandage off tomorrow. The reason I stayed back is that we have to talk. They caught the person who beat you up."

Detective Robinson came to the hospital and walked into the room. "How are you feeling, young man? The reason I am here is that I need to get a police report. I need to show you a photo for you to identify."

The boy said, "Yes, he's the one."

Detective Robinson asked, "Do you want to charge him?"

The boy said, "No, because I owe him money — $3,000."

Detective Robinson said, "We have to let him go. He will be back on the streets again. He is going to come back after you again. This is your last chance to talk. You need to do something very fast. If you need to call me, this is my card. Call me tomorrow."

The father said, "I will call you tomorrow."

To the son, he said, "You heard what Detective Robinson said. That bum will be back on the street. You need to think of something very fast."

The son said, "I will think of something by tomorrow."

The father said, "I will see you tomorrow. You will have a long day. Get some sleep. Don't forget what I said. Think about it."

The father arrived at home. The wife asked, "Can

we finish that talk?"

The father said, "Yes, our son is in a lot of trouble with a drug dealer. He owes the drug dealer $3,000. He didn't want to testify about the dealer. He will be back on the streets, the bum."

The wife said, "We have to do something fast because our lives could be in danger, too. Pay the money back. I have money saved. You never know what the drug dealer might do next. We are very happy he came out of the coma. The next time the drug dealer might kill our son. That's why we have to pay the money."

The father said, "We need to talk to him first before we pay the money. Tomorrow I have to pick him up at the hospital."

He arrived at the hospital the next day. The doctor said, "It's O.K. for him to go home. Good luck, young man."

The father asked his son, "How are you feeling?"

The son said, "I feel great, but I am a little nervous."

The father said, "We need to talk some more. Did you come to a conclusion about what you want to do?"

The son said, "Yes, I need to borrow $3,000 to get the drug dealer off my back."

The father said, "I told your mother."

The son yelled, "You told Mom! What did she say?"

The father said, "She wants to help."

Everyone was there to see him back home.

The son said, "Thank you for being here." They said

he was very lucky.

The mother and father said, "We have to talk. We both came to the agreement for you to pay the drug dealer back the money. You have to promise us you will never do this again. We are only doing it because we love you."

The son said, "Mom and Dad, I thank you so much. I will never let you down. I will pay you back, I promise."

The father worried whether he had done the right thing with his son.

The son thought, "I don't want to put pressure on my family any more. Maybe I should get some counseling for my drug problem. My father should talk to someone he can trust about this whole situation, even if I have to do some time in jail."

He said to the mother and father, "I want to do the right thing and turn my life around."

Church

Clifford Henry

The church choir singing

The air in the church

The coffee

The cake

The members

The spirit of the Lord

God is good

Carmen Hernandez

My Son Wants A Dog

Carmen Hernandez

When my son, Luis, was two years old, he asked me, "Can I get a dog?"

I said to him, "You should know that it's a big responsibility. I think that you should wait until you grow up so that you can get your pet and care for it."

But he never gave up asking.

When Luis was four, I went to the pet shop without my son. There were different kinds of dogs. Big dogs, little dogs, white dogs, black dogs. But I passed by the middle of the pet shop and saw a little brown dog. I said, "This is it, this is the one."

I chose the dog of his dreams. The dog has yellow eyes and a pointy nose. I will never forget the look on my son's face when I came back home with the little dog. I opened the car door and the doggy jumped out. Luis's expression was the most affected that I have ever seen in my whole life.

That was an experience so beautiful in our life. Now, Luis is nine years old. He continues loving his dog, "Chocolate," just as he did on that first day. He named the dog "Chocolate" because he said, "It looks like a chocolate bar!"

They are good friends. He always says, "I will never forget my first dog." He has memorable words such as this, which he has told me many times over.

This experience makes me feel proud of my son, Luis. He taught me a lesson, that age does not matter for a child to reach his dreams. Age does not matter for mothers, either. We must hold on to our dreams and never let go.

Cecilia Hunter is a student in the 1199SEIU Training and Employment Funds program in South Orange, NJ. Cecilia was born in Alabama. She has been here in Newark, NJ, for 30 years.

In My Room

Cecilia Hunter

The room needs to be decorated

The birds in my window

The freshness in my home

The food when I cook

The potatoes, onions, carrots before I cook them

The texture between them

It is going to be a really good soup!

Ray Irving is from Montego Bay, Jamaica. He is student in the 1199SEIU Training and Employment Funds program. He is trying to get his high school equivalency diploma. He loves to surf the web because there is so much to learn from the Internet.

A Bartender's Remedy

Ray H. Irving

Coming to the U.S from the Caribbean island of Jamaica was a journey of ups and downs. I started in the late 60's as a bar waiter aboard the MIS Starwar, one the ships operated by the Norwegian Caribbean Cruise line. It was hard at first, rough seas that I wasn't used to. I was seasick and I could hardly keep anything I ate down. I overcame it after drinking Compari and a little lime juice, which was a bartender remedy. I was fine in a blink of an eye.

After I was back to normal, which took about two months or so, I was transferred to a sister ship, the MIS Skyward. It was their newest in the fleet. I really miss all my friends I made and the weekly visit to my country, especially my home town of Montego Bay. The new ship was an upgrade. Our cabin was like the passenger cabins. This new accommodation came with a price: keep them clean and inspection was once a week. Each member that was assigned to the cabin had to pay a fine of $4.00 for repeated offenses which were not permitted. It was three strikes, and after that you lost your job. Not only your cabin, but the task assigned to you was inspected. The bars even were to be clean as well.

I was later promoted to chief of station, a position that was next to the bar manager. Although the new ship went on six-day cruises, they also made stops in Haiti, Trinidad, Barbados, Martinique, Saint Martin, Antigua, St. Thomas, and Puerto Rico. I still miss standing on the sun deck as it approached the port of Montego Bay, a modern pier with sometimes four ships in place, a backdrop with many waterfront resorts, beautiful white sand beaches, a lush hillside, and plenty of lovely houses and villas. It's picturesque, a scene that looks more beautiful every time I return.

Now I choose St. Thomas in the U.S Virgin Islands as my favorite scenery, because in many ways, it reminds me of the town of Montego Bay. They also served great food such as steamed fish with okra.

My journey is not finished, but has just begun. Now all I need is to receive my high school diploma to continue my journey. Who knows where it will take me!

Bianca Johnson is a student in the 1199SEIU Training and Employment Funds program in South Orange, NJ. She loves her family and she wishes the best for every single person. She also loves God. He is her reason for being alive.

Jamaica

Bianca Johnson

People buying things, walking back
and forth

Laughter and loud music

Taxi men being annoying

Burning bush and fresh rain

Wonderful food

Wonderful people

Fruits from the trees, dogs, the beach water

A sense of love from people that I don't
even know

Welcoming spirit

Jamaica is a wonderful place to visit or live.

Tammie C. Jones is the mother of five children and grandmother to one child. Her dream of obtaining her High School diploma came true in 2016 after enrolling in Essex County College's Adult Learning Center. Tammie Jones is entering her second semester at Essex County College, where she is studying to become a Registered Nurse. Tammie would also like to travel around the world.

Reaching My Goals

Tammie C. Jones

Allow me to introduce myself. My name is Tammie C. Jones and this is my second semesters at Essex College. I am so excited. I am a mother of five children and a grand-mom of one grandchild. When I was younger and growing up, my dreams were to become a Registered Nurse with a BSN degree and to travel around the world. My dreams of getting my high school diploma came true this year, 2016, at the Adult Learning Center at Essex County College.

Going back to school—it strengthens me to push myself more. To not give-up on my dreams. The College opened the doors of opportunity in my life. It gave me the ability that I can do all things through Christ, who empowers me to not give up on my dreams. Going back to school gave me the betterment for my children's future to not give up and stay focused on great things in life.

One day I would like to travel, but with the long hours at work and going to school, it will not happen soon. It took me twenty years of my life to finally get my high school diploma. What made me want to go back to school was my children and the job that I do. My two oldest sons had earned their high school diplomas, so I said to myself, "I can get my high school diploma, too."

The job that I do is a Nurse's Aide. I help and assist elderly clients. I have been in the nursing field since

1996, in Mankato, Minnesota, on again and off again. I am not satisfied with the job that I do, but I love caring for my residents. I thank the Lord for my job.

I had to encourage myself and say, "It's not too late to go back to school." I kept on going and coming to school, and I had to put up a good fight to stay focused and positive for my children, because I want better for them, too.

My oldest son is a National Guard member, and my second oldest son is in college in the Midwest studying to be an engineer. I said, God did it for my sons, God can do it for me to continue my education to stay in school to become a Registered Nurse.

That is my dream: to become a Traveling Nurse and travel the world.

Jainavoy Joseph is a student in the 1199SEIU Training and Employment Funds program in South Orange, NJ. He is from Haiti. He is the second child from a family of nine. Right now, he lives in NJ with a nice family, including parents and friends. Jainavoy loves his family.

Miami Beach Seaport

Jainavoy Joseph

People cruising the boats

They talk a lot about this place for their journey

Waves full of seafood

The water is so salty

The cool sea

I should be there every summer

Not easy because I moved to NJ

Juan Ling Li

Cooking Is Just Like Life

Juan Ling Li

My name is Juan Ling Li. I have an English name, Jenny.

I am from China. That is very far away from here. I miss my country, my family, my friends, and especially my mom's food.

I remember when I was nine years old, I saw my mom cooking many kinds of food for the Chinese New Year. When relatives came by, one by one to visit us, they ate the food. Everyone loved it. I did, too.

After the relatives left, I told my mom, "I want to learn to cook like you! I want you to teach me how to cook!"

When mom was cooking, I would stand near her and watch. Mom told me that cooking is a lot like other things you do: It needs love and patience. You must make each dish carefully, so that it will be the most delicious it can be.

A few days later I decided to make one of my favorite dishes. I gave it a name: "Sesame Fish." I bought one fresh fish, some garlic, some different kinds of pepper, and some vegetables. I took the food home. There, I cleaned the fish, washed the vegetables, and turned on the heat in the oven.

I put some oil in the pan and waited about five minutes. The oil became very, very hot. I put the fish in the pan to deep fry it. The oil splashed on my hand.

That hurt! But I still enjoyed cooking the fish.

I made the sauce, put the sauce on the fish and put sesame on top. Da-da-da, Sesame Fish was done.

I called my sister, brother, mom and dad to come try my fish. They each bit just a little piece of the fish, then they put down their chopsticks and drank a little water. They said, "It's good." But I knew they were just trying to pacify me, and that it wasn't really very good.

But I was am not giving up! In school, I cooked for my classmates. At home, I cooked for my family. At work, I cooked for my partner. I really enjoy cooking!

Twenty years later, I still remember my mom saying, "Take time, take patience, and carefully do everything with love."

It is true. Food is love with some seasoning and a little sauce.

i ♥ food.

Marilyn Louis is a student in the 1199SEIU Training and Employment Funds program in South Orange, NJ. She lives in Orange, NJ. She dedicates this poem to her children.

My Home

Marilyn Louis

My children every day

They laugh and play

The food that I cook

The book that I read

The love I have for my kids is very strong

I am a good mother

Ledia Lozanguiez: I want to finish school so I can show my daughter that having her didn't stop me from completing my goal of getting my high school degree. I am also doing this so I can become a state police officer. I desire to make my neighborhood safe again

Moment in Life

Ledia Lozanguiez
East Orange Adult Learning Program

Have you ever had a moment in life that made you laugh, cry or made you angry? Did you want to hold on to it or let it go? I'm thinking about a moment that I wish I could get back. This moment is so special to me because it's about someone near and dear to my heart, my mom. She really cared about me. I know she's in a better place but I still miss her.

Sometimes I cry and I'm always so angry because I feel like I lost not only my mom but my best friend. She helped me with everything. My mom was light skinned and kind of chunky, with long beautiful black hair. She took me everywhere she went. I loved being around my mom because she was a live spirit. Mother always loved throwing parties for me and doing my hair. She enjoyed taking me to school and picking me up from school as well. My mom liked having her family around, so she always hosted Thanksgiving and Christmas dinners for the whole family.

The moment my mom got sick, my worries started. She began throwing up, but my dad didn't take her to the doctors until it started happening more frequently. One day my dad came back from the hospital. I kept asking him, "Is my mommy okay?" He didn't want to tell me what was going on, so he said, "She's fine."

A couple of months passed and my mom was going to have surgery. I didn't know much about surgery, but now things started to change for me. My dad told me not to bother my mom. He gave me a house key and told me I'd have to walk to and from school by myself. This couldn't be good. Day by day my mom started getting worse. My brother would change mom's bandages and a nurse would be there at night and then again in the morning.

A few months had passed and the doctor alerted my dad that my mom probably would be gone by November. He shared this information with my aunt. Together they did what was necessary to make my mom's last days as comfortable as possible. A hospital bed was delivered and placed in the living room. Once that happened my dad broke down. My dad walked out crying and my aunt had to comfort him. He was having difficulty handling all these changes.

November 14th came. I was sleeping and my dad woke me and told me to move to my sister Ann's room while he checked on my mom. When he came back to my sister's room he told both of us that our mom had died. Next the pastor came, closed mom's eyes and prayed with us. My brother Karl dropped to his knees in tears. Everyone was crying while my mom's body was being carried out the door.

When I think of this moment all I want to do is cry. My mom, my best friend is gone. I feel as though of my two parents she was the easiest to talk to and she understood me more. She missed a lot of moments in my life up to now. I will recall this moment in time and I will always remember my loving mother. I wish she were here to see me now. I wish I had one more moment to tell her how much I love her.

Eli Mohammad

Landing in America

Eli Mohammad

One day, in 2013, I was 17 years old.

It was about 11:40 a.m. when the airplane I was in started decreasing its height, in order to land. The first things I saw were highways, houses, and large areas of trees. The houses looked so beautiful from the sky, and they were so organized, too. Trucks and cars looked so tiny. After a little while, I was disturbed by the flight captain's voice. He was providing us with some information about the time and weather in Newark.

After that, he said, "Please buckle up and get ready, we will land in 10 minutes."

At that moment I felt a kind of excitement mixed with a little fear, because I was about to experience something new, a place which is thousands of miles away from my homeland. At about 12:10 p.m., the plane's wheels hit the airport runway. That made a lot of noise and vibration, but everybody seemed to be happy and smiling. Finally, the plane arrived at the gate, and passengers started getting off of it. I didn't know anything, so I just followed them. A little bit later we arrived in a big room. There were long lines all the way around the front desks. The airport employees were checking some paperwork, which took some time. The airport was so big and full of nice perfumes from the newly arrived people. Luckily, I didn't get lost.

When I arrived at the main exit, my father was waiting for me, along with his friend. When he first saw me he started waving, laughing, and running toward me. He hugged and kissed me. I felt so good, like I was a child. I was so happy to see my dad again after a long three years. If someone you love has left, believe that you will see them again. Be sure of that, and never lose your hope and passion that one day you will be reunited.

Betania Rodriguez Rivas

The Beginning of my English Language

Betania Rodriguez Rivas

When I came to the United States, I did not speak English. The only language I spoke was Spanish, but in my country I always tried to learn some vocabulary in English.

That helped me to get a job in a supermarket working as a cashier, because at that time I knew the numbers in English, and also I knew some words. With the passing of time, trying to talk with the customers, I learned more vocabulary. And I was happy, because I was able to understand what people were saying. But I had a big problem.

When someone asked me certain questions in English, I felt nervous and I forgot everything I knew.

One day I went to the hospital with my husband and the doctor asked me a question, which was: "What is your relationship with him?"

I was nervous at first, but quickly answered him saying, "I am his Wi-Fi."

They were laughing, and my husband with a smile on his face said, "Give me the password please."

I thought that my answer was correct. But when we went home, my husband gave me a piece of paper and told me, "Write wife and Wi-Fi."

I wrote it correctly and I read it correctly, too. In that moment I knew my error with the doctor, and I never forget when someone asks me the same question.

But, I was interested in learning how to speak and write English well. That's was when I decided to come take the ESL class at Essex County College.

Since 2014, I feel that I am strongly improving my English. If you work hard and study hard and do everything with love, you can do anything you want. If you are not sure, use your Wi-Fi and go online.

Sharefah Robinson is a student in the 1199SEIU Training and Employment Funds program in South Orange, NJ. She lives in Newark, NJ and was born and raised in Irvington, NJ. She is currently on disability. Her goal is to get her High School Diploma and go to school to become an LPN.

My Great Grandmother's Kitchen

Sharefah Robinson

The smile on her beautiful face

The sound of pots and pans

Her homemade buttermilk biscuits in the oven

The softness of her buttery biscuits

My Grandmom when I give her a great big hug

The love whenever I was around her

I really miss my great grandmother a lot

And her cooking

Brianna Sanderson: After taking classes with the Fresh Start Academy High School, Brianna Sanderson has gone on to pursue other interests and challenges.

Moving Forward

Brianna Sanderson
Program: Fresh Start Academy High School

Let me introduce myself. My name is Brianna Sanderson. I am seventeen years of age. I was born in Newark, New Jersey. I have spent a large portion of my life with a single, yet amazing parent named Mitchelle Sanderson. Although I have only been on this earth for a brief time, I can tell you things have not always been smooth sailing. In fact, in such a short period of time I have suffered from major losses.

First, when I was only nine I lost my 18 year old brother to gang violence. My family and I were devastated to have lost a loved one at such a young age. He didn't deserve to die. I can recall my grandmother telling me he passed. I thought I was dreaming and this must have been a nightmare. I felt numb, shocked, empty, and I didn't want to believe the news.

His death had a terrible impact on me, he was the closest thing to me at that time.   I used to be a good student with straight A's and perfect attendance. Since his death, all of that changed. I was no longer focused. My grades have dropped and I didn't want to go to school. As a result, I am now in an alternative program trying to get my mind right and get back on track.

To add to my devastation, at the age of thirteen I

unexpectedly became pregnant and lost my child. Things seemed to go from bad to worse. I didn't even know I was pregnant. The first couple of weeks, I was nauseous and throwing up. Around that time I was thinking, "Could I be pregnant? But I discounted the idea. Young and foolish, I did not think to get a pregnancy test. As the weeks went on, I felt worse. I started bleeding uncontrollably. So at that point, I thought I couldn't be pregnant because I got my period. I wasn't concerned about being pregnant anymore, but I was certainly scared about the unusual amount of blood that kept pouring out of me.

After dealing with this bleeding for a few weeks, shockingly a baby came out of me on its own. I was so frightened, I had no idea what to do. I hadn't told anyone. I pushed this baby out into a pool of blood and held my dead baby in my hands. I started bawling my eyes out. I didn't know I was pregnant and now I'm all alone, looking down at my dead baby and blood is everywhere! It was truly a nightmare.

I decided it would be harder for me to tell anyone about the baby. I had already been going through a lot and was bullied by my own family and friends. I didn't want to disappoint them or have them judge me some more. I felt like I had to tell someone. This mistake could have cost me my life. I tried telling the father of the baby. He didn't believe me and laughed at me. He said I was crazy, but if it's true then I should get an abortion, a typical response from a young boy who's not ready to become a father.

I lived with this secret for some time. Finally, I decided to share what had happened with my mother and my family. When I told my family, their reaction was kind of shocking, but not surprising. My mom said I should have told her because I could have died. Other members were disappointed in me but agreed not to judge me as a "wanna be young and pregnant girl." But all in all, it went better than I had anticipated.

The moral of my story is, despite what I've gone through in life, I have come to realize that I deserve better for myself. I have experienced my brother's death and the death of my own child. I was in a relationship that ended badly. I've lost friends that were probably not my friends to begin with. I've been bullied by the best of bullies. I've made some bad decisions in life. Now, I'm turning the rest of my life around and doing what it takes for me to be happy and successful. I'm ready to put the past to rest and move forward. I'm going to get a GED. Someday, I hope to be a cosmetologist. As I'm doing a young girl's hair, I hope I can shed some glimmer of hope for her by sharing the do's and don'ts from my own life.

Rose Seelee is a student in the 1199SEIU Training and Employment Funds program in South Orange, NJ. Rose lives in Newark. She is from Monrovia/Liberia in West Africa. She has a 10 year old son and she would love him to become a physician and an evangelist. Her dream is to become a full-time pastor and to help the needy.

The Place Where I Was Born

Rose Seelee

A river that runs at the back of our house

The sound of frogs and crickets at night

The delicious breakfast my mom made

every morning

A delicious pepper soup and fu-fu made by

my mother

A pot of clay

The warm love of my mother

She's always with me

Chantal Sejour is a student in the 1199SEIU Training and Employment Funds program in South Orange, NJ. Chantal likes church. It is her number one priority besides her daily routine

My Church

Chantal Sejour

People coming in and out for prayer

The priest preaching about the Scriptures

The odor of the flowers

Some food after Mass for everybody to eat

A bottle of soda I want to drink but I can't

have caffeine

Disappointed. I really want a taste of it!

I know that if I drink it I will be sick to my

stomach.

Stanley Stewart is a proud veteran. He served in the United States army for three years. In his spare time, Stanley likes reading, baking and cooking. He also enjoys baking and delivering cookies to patients and staff at the VA hospital in East Orange, NJ. Stanley is a lifelong learner. He continues to enroll in classes at Essex County College (ECC) after completing classes at ECC's Adult Learning Center

Cooking For Life

Stanley Stewart, Jr.

I like to bake cookies in the morning. My favorite cookies are chocolate, oatmeal, raisin and peanut butter, especially with a glass of milk.

I like to bake my favorite cookies. I can eat them at breakfast and I can eat them at dinner, with milk or a glass of water. I bake them at a moderate temperature for eighteen minutes, then I take them out to cool for fifteen more minutes.

I learned to bake cookies in the army. I was stationed at Fort Knox, Kentucky. After I finished cooking school, I went to Viet Nam with the army. In Viet Nam I did a lot of cooking and cleaning, washing dishes and pots and pans, all the forks and knives and spoons. That was my service in the army. Serving and cleaning up for breakfast and lunch and dinner.

I spent my spare time reading and learning about food. It was hard work. I had a nervous breakdown and was in the hospital for eight months, at Walter Reade Hospital in Washington, DC. Finally I received an honorable medical discharge. I was given a 30% disability.

Today I am happy to use the skills that I learned in the military to cook and serve food, especially when I make my favorite cookies.

Neil Taylor I am 18 years old and I came to Fresh Start Academy to get my high school diploma. I am working very hard to earn my diploma and complete my goals. I won't stop working until I complete my education. Then, I would like to go to a trade school and study Heating Ventilation Air Conditioning and Refrigeration. Thank you for a second chance to do it all over

One Scary Moment in My Life

Neil Taylor

I am a 17 year old Jamaican boy who is about to share one of the scariest moments in my life. One sunny evening, my cousin and I were walking from school. We noticed a taxi driver's cab broken down on the highway. It was the same taxi that usually picks us up from school every evening, but now he was in need of a mechanic and we would have to make other arrangements. The evening was getting darker, so we decided to walk to our big cousin's Bun Bakery Factory. We would wait for him to finish working and then take a taxi home altogether.

By now, we were the only ones left on the school compound. So we started walking on the left side of the road one behind the other. We could actually see the Bun Factory, which was where we were headed. It had been really quiet while we were walking, neither one of us had much to say. Suddenly, out of nowhere, I heard a loud thump and a piercing, screeching noise from a car's wheels. It frightened me so much I started screaming and quickly spun around to see what was happening. It was my little cousin spinning on the top of a car hood. When the driver of the car hit the brake pedal, my cousin flipped from the hood and was tossed on the ground in front of the car. Finally, the car stopped and the driver jumped out, asking my cousin if he's OK.

I started freaking out and trembling with fear. I, too, ran over to my cousin. I brushed my hand over the top of his head and asked, "What happened?" He didn't seem to know what happened either, because he asked me what had happened. I said, "Why are you asking me, I wasn't the one who got hit by the car."

He started crying and I couldn't help from shedding my own tears.

Next the man picked my cousin up and took us over to the hospital. He asked me, "Do you have a number for his parents or guardian?" I answered, "Yes, I do, sir." He was a nice gentleman. In the back of the man's car I was staring into space, feeling a bit weak myself. When we reached the hospital we called my cousin's mom. My aunt arrived at the hospital quickly, crying hysterically. The police came and asked lots of questions. My cousin was admitted to the hospital that night but, miraculously, was released the next day. He said he was feeling great. I was relieved.

This was truly the scariest moment in my life. My cousin could have died! When my cousin came home from the hospital our family and some members of the community gathered to pray for him. They begged him to give his life to the Lord and become a Christian.

Despite what had happened, he said he couldn't manage the life of a Christian at his young age, he wasn't ready to give up his ways and the dirty words that came from his mouth. However, he does go to church and reads his bible, he just can't stop using bad words. He says maybe when he's about 22 and wants to get married and settle down, then he'll commit to becoming a Christian. Even to this day, my aunt cries and prays for my cousin. She warns him to stay out of trouble. She believes he has been given another chance at life, and as a result he should give the rest of his life to GOD. His near death experience was the scariest moment in my life.

Sandra Thomas is a student in the 1199SEIU Training and Employment Funds program in South Orange, NJ. She was born in Jamaica, West Indies. She is the sixth of nine children. She is presently working as a private duty nurse. Sandra is the mother of five children and five grandchildren. Her hobbies are reading, cooking and praying.

Jamaica, West Indies

Sandra Thomas

White sand beaches with blue water

Native reggae music playing

Aroma of jerk chicken in the air

So many familiar foods I enjoyed as a child

Donating towards education to touch other

people's lives

Sad sometimes

It reminds me of my grandmother's passing

Someday I will retire there

Nazeen White is a student in the 1199SEIU Training and Employment Funds program in South Orange, NJ. Nazeen was born in Jamaica, West Indies. She is married with four kids.

Jamaica

Nazeen White

Hummingbird's sweet sound in the air

Cool breeze blowing

People walking by

Beautiful flowers

My mother's cooking

Rice and peas, brown stew, jerk chicken,

curry goat

All the memories coming back to me

My beautiful country, Jamaica

BUY OUR FIRST BOOK
at AMAZON!

Connections through Expression
A Collection of Memoirs, Poetry
and Intrigue
by Essex County Consortium Students
Judith Celestin (Editor)
(https://tinyurl.com/lnnqhp8)

CONNECTIONS
THROUGH EXPRESSION

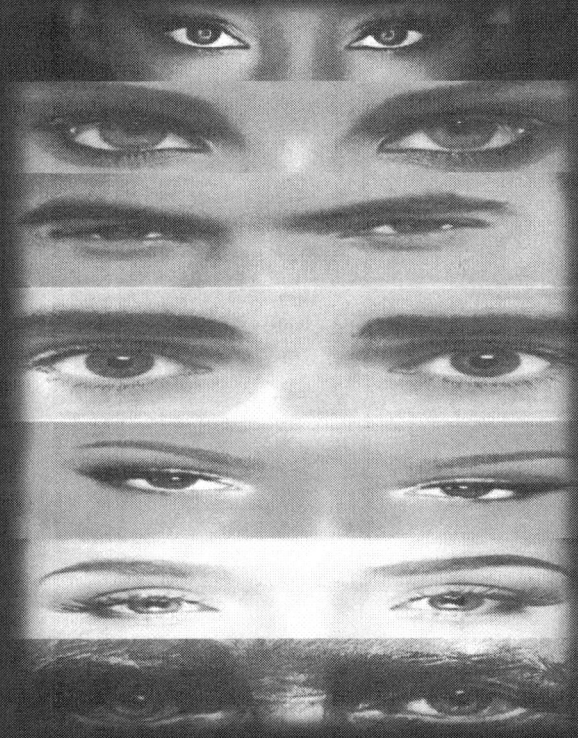

A COLLECTION OF MEMOIRS,
POETRY AND INTRIGUE

BY THE ESSEX COUNTY CONSORTIUM STUDENTS
EDITED BY JUDITH CELESTIN AND ELLEN RAY

69885562R00089

Made in the USA
Columbia, SC
29 April 2017